WORTH MORE
THAN YOU KNOW

Martha Okwuokenye

Copyright © 2021 Martha Okwuokenye

All rights reserved. No part of this publication may be reproduced, distributed, or transmitted in any form or by any means, including photocopying, recording, or other electronic or mechanical methods, without the prior written permission of the publisher, except in the case of brief quotations embodied in critical reviews and certain other noncommercial uses permitted by copyright law.

Paperback ISBN: 9798500719348
eBook ISBN: 978-1-63616-029-0

Published by Opportune Independent Publishing Company

For permission requests, write to the publisher, addressed "Attention: Permissions Coordinator" to the address below.

Email: Info@opportunepublishing.com

Address: 113 N. Live Oak Street
Houston, TX 77003

DEDICATION

To God, who looked upon me with mercy even when I don't deserve it. I am grateful Lord because I am absolutely nothing without you. To my supportive and patient husband, the father of my lovely kids, you are my hidden strength. To my family, thank you all for believing in me.

ACKNOWLEDGMENT

I will like to express my special thanks to God Almighty. To my husband, Daniel Okwuokenye, my children, Michael and Jaydan, and my niece, Nkechi Moteh, who believed that I could achieve this with no doubt. To my siblings and my friend, Latesia Thomas, who each continually encourages me to push harder. To my prayer warrior and the best mother-in-law, Felicia Okwuokeneye, thanks for all of your encouragement.

LIVING YOUR
FULL
POTENTIAL

INTRODUCTION

Many people wonder what their potential is.

What does it mean to live your full potential?

How do you recognize your potential?
Do you have potential?
If you do have potential, then how do you achieve it?
Why are you here (purpose)?

When you start to think of your potential, many questions can pop up at that time, which may be confusing. Then you find yourself stressed out and wandering around in deep thought. At that point, you should take a moment to focus on yourself and realize the extraordinary things that are unique about you - the gift or talent you have that can't be replaced. Focus on your capability and what you can actually do. Doing so will motivate your determination to be successful in life. It's important to know who you are and your purpose of existence.

We are in a world where we are easily distracted with things around us, stress and frustration of life, focus on your dreams and goals.

Its so disappointing that in the society we are in today, an average person has no idea who they are, what they are called or destine to accomplish, which is the source of everything that happens to you and the things that you face in life. It's so powerful that you absolutely need to know in order to live your full potential and you will be motivated each day.

Believe in yourself and have faith that the best in you is yet to be discovered, and that it will be revealed in no time. You are more powerful than you think! So when striving to become someone with great value in life, or pursuing your potential, you need to be courageous and believe that it can be achieved with no doubt. Don't just imagine it, but actually believe it as well with everything inside you.

Only then can you fully fight obstacles that may pin you down. Your potential is a priceless treasure that is hidden inside, you must strive to dig it out yourself. You have the tools and energy to do so; no one can help you, no matter how close or caring they are to you. Believe in yourself and focus on one thing at a time and make it a priority. Once you get that down, your life will no longer be the same again.

No matter how many times you fail or are rejected, if you are trying to discover your real purpose, you can't stop pushing harder to achieve this.

Remember there is no competition in discovering who you are or what you are made of, your current situation does not define your ultimate potential in life. It's never too late to rise up and pursue this gift, God is too faithful to leave you halfway.

I will be helping you with ways to recognize your potential. This has always been my heart's desire - to lead others into getting energized from doing what they like best to achieve success in life. No matter who you are or your family background you have a potential that can not be hidden.

I grew up in an environment where every day was a struggle to make ends meet. Waking up each day not knowing what the day holds was really hard. There were struggles to put food on the table, look normal like your peers, and to be able to meet the standard of simple living. Getting an education was very difficult as well because there were no resources, or anyone to help lift that poverty status off.

We all face many different obstacles, but once you understand the power of your potential, you will keep pushing to actualize anything.

You need to be determined to achieve your purpose in life; you have a prophetic destiny from God when he said before you were born, I knew you. He made you with his likeness, and the enemy knows what you are made of, and is trying to convince you that you are nothing but a failure. You need to stand up with a declaration that you are not a failure, and nothing will stand as a circumstance to achieving your goals.

Each day, new issues may arise like hardship, sickness, unpleasant situations, frustrations, etc., because the enemy knows if you are free of worry, that you will overshadow. Remember, as we said earlier that these types of situations are just stepping stones to getting you ready to achieve your great purpose. In order for you to succeed in life, you must be stressed and tempted to quit at some point or another. Stress is God's way of training you. No one likes stress, but it is absolutely necessary at times.

I was an inspiration to myself, struggling each day with the expectation that I must unveil my real self, and I believed, to some of the people who had the opportunity to be around me, were also inspired.

At the age of eleven, I lost my dad, and my mother had no hope for tomorrow. All of her kids were still pretty young and all lived under someone else's care. My mother was unemployed and uneducated, so instead of finding a careered job, she had to settle for the usual farming gigs. I was the only person living with my parents when this unfortunate circumstance arose, my first fearful thoughts were how would I survive and how would I achieve my dream life?

Not only did I lose my dad, but I was also attacked spiritually.

One day, I woke up and experienced the most tragic thing ever. I stood up, as usual, to start my morning routine and realized that I couldn't move my legs nor turn my neck. I remember it sounded like a comedy movie when I screamed, calling for help. The people that heard my voice came to rescue me as I was still crying and yelling.

I recall not feeling any pain but I could not move my body, everyone around me tried to figure out what caused this sudden illness. My mother had gone to the farm only to return home to find me helpless and bed ridden. I kept speaking out these words of encouragement, "God, my life is for a purpose, I know you are with me, and nothing happens to any of your children without your knowledge."

I struggled with being bed ridden and handicapped for over two years before I was able to walk again, and although I am still struggling, God has given me peace. You may be reading this from the hospital, sick bed, or in a state of depression please just listen to God, and don't give up when you are feeling weak and it seems you cannot move forward. Remember Isaiah 40:31, "But they that wait upon the LORD shall renew their strength; they shall mount up with wings as eagles; they shall run, and not be weary; and they shall walk, and not faint."

I know what it feels like to lose hope and this is why I am encouraging you today to pursue your goals. Don't allow your dreams to die, don't give any excuses, make determination your daily nutrition, and never be afraid or underestimate your ability. Great people don't allow their dreams to die... They live for their dreams. When the opportunity arises, grab it with both hands.

Be an example to people around you and be willing to help passionately because
It's known that in the process of helping others in pursuing their goals or potential, many discover their own. There is nothing more rewarding than inspiring someone else on their journey of self-discovery.

/pəˈten(t)SHəl/

THE ABILITY TO DEVELOP SOMETHING THAT MAY LEAD TO SUCCESS IN THE FUTURE.

HAVING POTENTIAL IS THE ABILITY OR QUALITY TO BECOME SUCCESSFUL.

POTENTIAL

You will live in your full potential when you start having a positive outlook and having the passion for pursuing your goals. Living in your potential will minimize the stress that comes along with challenges. When you constantly zealous about learning and making progress. You won't mind working hard towards your goals.

Start by knowing yourself, your strengths and your weaknesses.

What do you like doing?
Which activities do you truly enjoy?
What brings you happiness and inspire you?

There are few things you can do to help you reveal your true self:

1. Be courageous! Don't fill yourself with negativity. Oftentimes we get discouraged about ourselves because of our failed experiences or circumstances, especially listening and paying attention to what others may say about us. You need to have the courage to face your fears, focus on doing your best, and learn from any mistake or error that might surface.

Often times, we hear about someone who has so much potential but is wasting it. We are really quick to talk about someone and judge them by what we see.

We have a huge role to play in our society, especially when we recognize individuals who have so much potential and are ignorant to their gifts. We need to stand up and speak, work to help these individuals achieve their goals. I believe everyone has a light that they carry, and that light is your destiny. We need to let that light comfort us through pushing harder.

2. Observe your feelings. Stop for a minute, take a deep breath and reconnect with yourself. Focus on the positive things first - the things that give you good memories.

3. Set out a challenge for yourself and put your best effort towards it. Just like someone who has an interest in cooking, they bring couple of Ingredients together and make a delicious dish out of it, People

will be excited and ready to have a taste of that very special recipe. This is an example of unveiling potential.

4. Work on your attitude and let go of any bitterness. People are often discouraged by things that have happened to them, the environment they live in, society, and their background. We have so many reasons for our limitations or the reason why we haven't achieved our goals or living in our full potential. We should not allow these limitations to speak for us.

5. Pay more attention to what people say about you whenever you do something extraordinary. Oftentimes we may receive a lot of credit or compliments for things we've done that have led us to success, but we never have the time to dwell on the achievement.

Ask yourself the following questions:
How did I get here?
How did I achieve this?
What are the things I should have done differently?

Be excited about your success and failures because they will build your strength. Be confident about yourself as your experiences will boost your continued success. Even when you have a disappointing moment, remember all of the times you've tried and know that your victory is around the corner. Don't have a fixed mindset or be discouraged about things when they don't work out as planned. Have an open mind and try new things. Life is a learning process, be ready to fail and rise as failure is part of success.

Be honest with yourself and get better at pursuing your goals. You need the spirit of excellence which is a daily process and consistency to accomplish these goals. Let your desire to be excellent motivate you that even your children will have the opportunity to reach their full potential by following your example. Don't strive to be perfect but instead strive to be successful and strive for excellence.

You are a seed from God and made in his likeness. Your potential is limitless, so challenge your limitation and be thankful for what you have, and you will end up having more.

Push yourself as if there's no limit to what you can achieve. Don't let anyone discourage or define you, know that only you can define yourself. Stop getting confuse about yourself in no time everything will work out for good' Of course the system tends to judge people by tests and performance, and if you fail, they say you are not smart. Take total control of your life and destiny! Let no one predict your intelligence, so never settle by how they see or judge you.

God knows when to send you exactly what you need to get started and no one else can do it for you. Create a plan and make it a priority. If your plan doesn't work, change the plan, not the goal. No one wants to live a life full of regret or live a life not knowing their purpose.

Don't move wherever the winds blow you to' have a direction and purpose. Some people will make a mockery of you intentionally, just laugh over it. Step out of your comfort zone and make this life-changing decision today. You cannot settle for less; you deserve more out of life in this moment and you are worth more than you know.

Let your story inspire someone. You are unstoppable, not because there weren't any challenges, failures, stress or obstacles, but because you never allowed it to withhold you.

Life goes by so fast and faster than we think, so why wait and give an excuse?

Don't give up! Great people don't give up on their goals. Remember, all dreams can come true if you have the courage to pursue them. Make your life a masterpiece and have control over it. You will be disappointed each time you fail, but it is a step ladder to success. Remember, every disappointment or weakness you have is an opportunity for God to show up, he has promised he is with us, stay focused and determined to get this desire accomplished with no limitation.

Everyone is born with a great seed. All you need to do is to plant those seeds and water them each day with hard work, and they will eventually germinate, and the end product will surprise you. God is great, and he made us in his greatness. We are the product of greatness. Remember, you don't have to be a Christian to believe that you have great seed in you.

Another great decision is to NEVER share your dreams with negative people who tell you it can't be done— people who never see good in others and give a million reasons why you won't make it. You need to disassociate yourself from those foes. There's no need to waste your time with unprofitable conversations. Determine who you spend most of your time with and the things or activities you choose to engage in.

Don't allow your environment or your family to determine what you'll become in life. You have all it takes to live your best life and be an inspiration. It's not too late, don't die with an unused gift that God has given because you must account for it.

I grew up in a house of seven children and I am the only person who pursued a college education. I had a burning desire to make my dream-life a reality. I went through the process and even when I lost my confidence I still didn't give up. The picture was clear—I am destined for greatness. Although my physical circumstances stood as a limitation, I chose not to give up. I was confident things were going to be okay, and God always shows up when we most need him.

GOD
IS
TOO
FAITHFUL

TO
FAIL

God is too faithful to fail, these words are so prolific and powerful, and there must be a lot of trust and faith for one to proclaim them. It requires believing and having confidence that God is faithful even when you don't see it. Often times, we hear people say, "Great is your faithfulness." Oh Lord, God never fails, and his mercy is new every morning, we proclaim this all of the time, and that is the reality of who God is. He is a great and unfailing God. Even when we don't deserve God's love, he is still faithful to us. He never takes his eyes off us for a moment. 2 Timothy 2:13 says "If we are faithless, He remains faithful. He cannot deny himself".

Some of the things we go through each day in life sometimes make us question our faith and wonder if God is still really who he says he is; no doubt this is just a way to direct our path into a perfect stage. God teaches us in many ways how to understand who he is. He hears every unspoken word and sees every unseen wound. You just have to believe and stay strong.

Psalm 73:26 tells us that "My flesh may fail, but God is the strength of my heart he is mine forever."

Each day you should feed your mind with the fact that when God makes a promise, he is going to fulfill it; even when your faith is being tested, and it looks like your prayers are not being answered. When nothing is working out the way you planned, everyone around you is successful and living their best life, and you are left with the question, "Is God really who he said he is?"

You may feel frustrated, and a negative mood continuously overwhelm you. You believe in him but can't physically see it because of the circumstances surrounding you. Just remember, God is truthful when he said he is faithful. God cannot violate his personality or mislead us; he is there in every circumstance. We need to always keep believing and proclaiming his faithfulness, and he will never leave or forsake us.

He promises to always be with you. He will protect you, be your strength, answer you, and he will provide for you. GOD promises to give you his peace, these are his words of assurance, and he is the same God today, and forever. God said that heaven and Earth shall pass away, but his words must be accomplished.

Never regret a day in your life, as good days gives us happiness and fills our hearts with gratitude, bad days gives us a great experience. Often times, we may focus more on the things that hurt us or when things didn't work out for us. Don't let the failure of yesterday ruin your today or allow your yesterday to take much of your today.

Life goes on whether you choose to move on and take a chance to make today a better day, or choose to stay behind your past. You need to leave the past and start focusing on the greatness of today. A small step in the right direction can turn out to be the biggest step of your life and the right time to take that step is today.

HAVING CONTROL
OVER YOUR ANGER

Anger is a big setback and an enemy to one's happiness. It's a strong emotion that you feel when something frustrates you or makes you feel sad. It's a sign that something has to change. Instead of causing unhealthy trauma, recheck yourself and see if you are the one who needs the change.

Sometimes we are the cause of the thing that angers us.

Remember, anger doesn't solve anything but can destroy what you have built over time. Realistically, it's really very difficult to control one's temper when this unimaginable feeling comes.

Occasionally, we may experience so much pressure and stress from life that causes so much anger and unhappiness, but we should never allow it to have total control over us. Be the remote controller of your emotions. Feed your mind with positive thoughts and engage in meaningful activities that will attract great attitudes.

Remember, no one is perfect and no one is an exception to anger. It can occur anytime, but the difference is how we react to it. This is why there are stages in life that allow us to grow physically, emotionally, and spiritually in a perfect direction.

Be happy, stay happy and make happiness the key factor of your daily life.

Anger is a sign of frustration and love. You feel anger because you care about something. When things don't go well in our direction, we tend to get upset and angry. It's okay to feel angry about something, but don't let anger take control over you. Being angry is a normal way for a human to express their hurt feelings. Forget what hurt you in the past because you can't take it back, but never forget the lessons you learned from it. Learning from your past hurt will help you build very strong unshakable emotions.

God allows some things to happen to us just to test our faith, and also to let us see our weaknesses. He uses the worse things done to you to bring out the best in you.

Sometimes you need bad things to happen to inspire you.

Honestly, in life, not being offended is unachievable and unrealistic; it's impossible to escape being offended. This is what you must experience in life, both in your family, marriage, job, and from people who you love.
You will be insulted, betrayed, embarrassed, and humiliated, but you must remain humble and sweet at all times and allow God to take over you. Condition your mind that sooner or later this will happen, so your reaction to it is a reflection of you. Stay unshaken and stop crying for the old days.

MOST COMMON CAUSES OF ANGER

- Personal issues, both physical and mentally
- Relationship difficulties
- Poverty
- Temperament
- Stress
- Lack of faith or trust
- Impatient, especially when in traffic and a hurry

Anger is a serious enemy to the soul. It has a way of bulling you and subjecting you to a life full of fear, anxiety, depression, and unhappiness.

People get angry easily because of the fear of the unknown, fear of failure, and frustration. When you see yourself angry and obviously can't control the situation or what is happening, challenge yourself to control your response. Your soul gets troubled whenever you are angry. You need to be emotionally balanced, so when someone makes you angry, it won't move you into reacting.

God is faithful to allow this unhealthy circumstance to define you. Each time you find yourself being angry, smile and take a deep breath. DON'T get too hung up with emotions that will push you into reacting negatively. Don't let anyone make you lose control, be slow to speak when you are upset and speak positivity.

Don't react immediately, this may lead to total regret. People will always offend you, both intentional and unintentional, just as we may offend others without knowing. We need to understand the simple principle of happiness and let it overflow the enemy (ANGER).

MAKE HAPPINESS A PRIORITY

This is a personal effort, no one can make you happy and it's totally up to you and completely your own decision. The moment you decide to put all hope in someone else to make you happy in life, be ready to experience disappointment.

No one can ever make you happy, they might do things that make you happy which could or may expire one day, but the total happiness of your life depends on you. So make yourself a priority, and stop trying to impress others.

Be yourself, love yourself and be happy for yourself. The moment you feel unhappy, just remember there's someone who is living because of you, and you can't afford to disappoint them. As my husband would say, "Happiness is a choice." Whenever I am mad and I feel like bringing down heaven and crashing down walls, I begin to complain about how life has been frustrating, unfair and how people have treated me badly. I always remember this is a choice.

It could be because things didn't go my way or disappointment In general. Sometimes I will go days without speaking to anyone, reject food, and even lose sleep over things that I had the choose to let go of and move on. The people who upset you are living their life and going about their day joyfully. You may experience sadness and anger however, the way you react to it is completely a choice. Choose happiness and make it a priority.

I have a personal issue of putting everyone else first in my life and forgetting that my first responsibility is making myself happy. Most times, we lose the importance of who we are while trying to impress others. Yes, you can't give out what you don't have. If you need people around you to be happy, you need to be happy yourself and quit living like the whole world is against you.

I have always struggled with the fear that my life will crumble once the people I loved and looked up to pissed me off. Sometimes, they ignore me no matter what I do to draw attention. I would cry day and night just because someone refused to speak with me. I remember I would call friends and family members just to explain and justify my feelings and the reason I am being treated badly. Not knowing that the more you expose yourself to different people, the more opportunity the enemy has to implant negativity in you.

Each time you explain your agony and disappointment, you are actually looking for justice and sympathy, which will actually lead to losing self-respect. The more upset your spirit is, the more people will give you their own opinion on how you deserve the best, and offer all kinds of solutions.

The fact remains you do not need any emotional drama or stress. You represent God and you are a reflection of him, so let your attitude attract good things and that is Godly. You can't allow anyone to bring you down or steal your joy.

Having considered all of these factors that anger can cause, we need to choose happiness to overcome this fear and torture.

A happy life is a healthy life. We have the choice to live our life filled with happiness even when the challenges that anger throws on us get harder, and it seems we are losing all we have and hoped for. You have to be strong and realize that being angry over every frustration is never the solution.

Life may have thrown a lot of unimaginable scars at you, leaving you wondering if everything is still going to be okay. You live each day with a lot of questions that have no answers. I encourage you today to stand firm and be courageous.

Don't give up on yourself, smile through it and keep pushing. We have an unfailing God who cares and watches over us. Some of the things that caused this anger may be the outcome of what we outlined earlier, but remember, we still have the key to controlling how we allow these feelings to get to us.
I have been in a situation so many times where I allowed anger to make decision for me, and that has left me with total regret. I have since moved on and learned from this experience. I do not dwell on the regret because that is an enemy to the soul. It continually reminds you of your failure and your bad attitude. People will misunderstand you and

sometimes take your kindness for granted. Just be calm and don't take things personally.

On several occasions, I have struggled with breaking down just because of how I have been treated. People tend to lash out their frustration on others without any sense of emotion, which hurts.

Life's struggle has stressed so many that they no longer care about others feelings. I noticed even when I go out of my way to please people, making sure their happiness becomes a part of me, it all ends up making me miserable because they don't appreciate it. Each time I try harder, I am always misunderstood, and it doesn't feel good.

I remember helping a walk-in customer who didn't have an appointment, but I was moved to help, and I offered my assistance. It took me about an hour to get everything done for her. I sacrificed the next appointment scheduled to accommodate her, which of course was not an acceptable thing to do. After helping her and her husband, she left happy, and I felt so good that I was able to make someone smile at the moment they most needed it.
A few days later, I got a call that someone was on the phone for me.

"Hello," I spoke and was expecting a response.
It was a customer. "Yes, this is Mrs... The lady you helped the other day."

I responded, "Oh, how are you doing?"

The customer said, "I am calling because I need to speak with your supervisor or anyone higher than you. You got the guts to mess up my account and block me from using my account, which is unacceptable, and you must be fired and face disciplinary action."

She was cursing and verbally abusing me, she wouldn't listen to me for a minute, I remember all I could say was, "Ma'am, I did not do it, this was not me."

She went on and on, so I offered for her to speak with my manager. I transferred the call to my manager, but she still wasn't satisfied, insisting I was to blame. The bank system had all records of every change she had on her account, the date, time and who caused the changes. We discovered that she called the bank a few weeks before coming to me for assistance and advised her information was stolen. She requested a block on her account for which we have all of the conversations recorded.

My point here is that I was humiliated, insulted, accused and threatened to be fired just for going out of my way to please somebody. I broke down, wept, and asked God why? What is my offense? What did I do wrong to deserve this humiliation? The answer is LOVE. I was able to hold back, and I never allowed my emotions to make the decision at that time. It does not matter what they did to you, or what life may have done to you, just keep the right spirit, and God will give you peace.

Just as God forgives and never holds back on our disobedience, we should never hold back on the things that angers us.

We are in a generation where some people may feel their opinion and voices are never heard, or they have never been given the opportunity to express themselves. They feel frustrated and angry. Don't try to defend yourself by fighting and being moved by your emotion to react negatively. Worse is ending up being imprisoned by things you have no idea about.

Some have lost their lives, loved ones, and all of the things they hoped for just for situations like this, but in the midst of this so many have scaled through. Counting on these circumstances will give you a million reasons to remain sad and be angry for as long as they exist. You need to love as if you have never been hurt, be calm even though you have been wounded and your glory and honor will come back, your respect will be restored. Don't get angry and seek revenge because God will let your reputations grow back. Remember, love and happiness with sweet words break the spirit of anger, also staying around people with a positive attitude and a great mindset can help. If people begin to accept the fact that they really have made a mistake and learn from it, their life will be great. The moment you accept the responsibility for everything that happens to you is the moment you gain the power to change everything in your life. You can't go back to change the beginning, but you can start where you are and change the ending with the help of God. For with God, all things are possible.

Maybe you have given up on making happiness a healthy life choice because of anger, frustration, and anxiety. Today is a new day, stand up and make happiness a priority no matter the circumstance. I believe in being strong even when everything seems to be going wrong. Let's put the anger behind us - where it belongs. When we conquer our anger and fear, things will definitely begin to fall in place for us. By you getting healthier, you will start noticing your physical looks will begin changing and glowing. Start creating a life that you love that will inspire people around you. After all of that, success will be inevitable in the end. Happiness changes everything. It gives you peace of mind and even a healthy relationship with the people around you; remember, happiness is free.

Seek the spirit of excellence; it's a habit, not an accident. Excellent behavior is the result of your intentions. Let it be of good and clear intention, don't seek revenge because someone disrespected you or betrayed you. Push yourself to be better, have a great attitude, and do ordinary things in an extraordinary way. We become what we repeatedly do. Whether good or bad, it becomes a reflection of you. That is why it's called a habit.

LOVE

The word love is complex. It's a strong feeling of affection between one another; to love is to be passionate. When someone loves and has compassion for another, they have an understanding of what the other person is going through. True love care about others welfare and the way they live. When you love and care about something, you nurture it, feed it, pay attention to its existence and your actions will reflect it.

Love is a strong emotion that must be expressed in a unique way. It's showing affection towards one another, and it's not limited to your spouse, children, family members, or close relations.

God shows us love, even when we don't deserve it. His sacrifice at the cross was a real definition of love, and it's unconditional. He didn't wait for us to be perfect to then show us his love. He said, "It's my commandment that you should love one another just as I have loved you." (John 15:12)

God is love and anyone who loves God must love one another

Recently I started wondering if people will actually start loving one another just as GOD loves and cares for us; the world would be a better place. A place where there's no room for hate and jealousy, no room for racialism or hatred. A place where you don't have to worry about your life being cut short just because someone dislikes you and the color of your skin. A place where you find peace and security and loyalty is standard.

Life is precious, and we need to handle it preciously and live with one another in peace and harmony

Love is when you are eating, and you remember that there is someone out there who doesn't have the opportunity to feed their family with just one square meal a day. Knowing this, you feel as if you have to share your meal with these people. It's making sacrifices even when it is not convenient for you. You should always be willing to support and help someone to make a difference, sharing in their daily struggle and happiness. Their success becomes a priority for you.

Everything you are going through is a process to getting to your destiny. You need to be patient while you wait, as love is patient.

I encourage you to love and love unconditionally. Go out for outreach, be a blessing today to someone who has lived all their life knowing or feeling no one loves them. You may not have always felt loved all of your life but do not let those feelings distract you from showing love to those who need it. Love is a beautiful thing, and there are different ways to show love to one another. You can show your love by sending a gift, sharing in their pains and listening to their voices, and by paying attention to their needs, their life will be changed, goals and purpose achieved, dreams comes through, if we as people will start showing love and care to those who has lost hope ' this world will be a better place

Little do you know that just a simple 'I love the way you dress' or complimenting someone's hair can go a long way in making someone feel special and loved. Write a note and leave it around someone's work desk, car, or even a restroom.

As far as your spouse, think about what they enjoy or spend most of their time doing? My husband spends a lengthy time in our restroom and enjoys dressing his hair, so I decided to leave a remarkable, loving, and life-changing note on his mirror and on the restroom door. I also recently figured out since he spends a lot of time in the restroom that I could decorate it in a unique way just for him to feel more relaxed. He loved it; he never asked for it, just a way of showing how much I care and appreciate him. This Might not be a big deal to many, but it was designed with his favorite things. My point here is nothing is too small' when showing someone how much you care and appreciate them

It's important to show love, even when life isn't going perfectly.

According to James Keller, "A candle does not lose anything by lighting another candle, so it's absolutely important to show love at all times, never hate." Or Jealous, rather be an example of love, be willing to open up your heart.

Forgive and be kind, God loves us and instructs us to love one another in life. You need to have a reason for what you are doing, which should be the things that you are passionate about. Make a decision today to be a blessing to someone who is in need out there today, do not be discouraged by the circumstance surrounding you. Do not let anybody who has no idea about the divine spirit make a decision for you.. There are so many souls out there who are waiting for your gift of love to be lifted. You don't have to be rich or influential to show love.

I was once told by someone that I respect a lot, Brother Seun, "Never let people change the loving person that you are, don't let anyone get you down no matter the challenges you may have experienced."

Use the love and goodness inside of you to stay strong. Be who you are and know that you cannot be duplicated. It's a great choice to be a loving person, you become a better person by caring for and loving others.

If you have the chance to make somebody happy, just do it without procrastinating and make them feel like they are special today. Do not expect anything in return because that is where you may get disappointed. Love is priceless and one of the greatest gifts anyone can give.

Remember, when you truly love someone, their mistakes never change your feelings towards them because it's the mind that gets hurts, but the heart still loves and cares.

PATIENCE
IN TIMES OF TRIALS

Human nature tends to react impatiently when things don't go the right way, but we need to be patient amid that frustration. Having patience is very challenging, it takes a lot of sacrifice to fight your emotions, but at the same time it's easier to deal with compared to being stressed out over things you can't control.

Patience is having the ability to tolerate those things that trouble and upset you without getting angry. You endure these emotions in a calm and less stressful way. Even when you have been waiting forever to get through it, you remain unprovoked, showing this quality of compassion and endurance. This has a great impact on our health. When we are patient, we can overcome stress and challenges in a better way without getting stressed. Patience is the antidote to an unhealthy lifestyle.

My life did not change overnight. I experienced so much and waited long for my change and growth, both physically and emotionally. GOD prepared my development through perseverance and trust. I learned how to trust him and hoped patiently that one day my life would change for the better. The process is very uncomfortable and bitter, but the fruit is sweet. Sometimes being patient may sound, or make you look stupid but this will shape and help you develop the right attitude. Seek to have a day filled with peace, love, kindness, and self-control during the time of trials and suffering.

Personally, I have been asking God for patience repeatedly. Each time I tried to exercise patience, it always messed me up because I take things so personally. This kept hurting me emotionally and stressing me out, and of course, it also affected me physically. Nothing was able to bring me happiness, I was always unhappy and sad. I lacked patience and when things weren't done right, it bothered me badly, but God always has a way of reminding us of how unrighteous we are.

When you are tempted to lose patience with someone, think of how patient God has been with you, all of the time, each day. We live a life of disobedience and he still forgives and never gets back at us. You have all it takes to be the best and live life stress-free. Once you get closer to God, just relax, and everything will fall into place. All things are difficult before they become easy, even the simplest things like learning your ABCs. Today I am grateful to God for his mercy, grace and patience for all the times I failed. God hasn't let me go, He never stops, no matter how many times it takes.

LET YOUR DESIRE EACH DAY BE

Dear God, if I'm wrong in my words and actions, please correct me, when I am lost in deep sin, and confusion guides me.

If I start to give up on myself and fill with negativity, Lord, please keep me going.

It's time to forget the past and forget your mistakes and focus more on what he is doing today.

The pruning process can be uncomfortable and painful, but it is all for your good.

IMPORTANCE OF PATIENCE

Philippians 4:6, "Do not be anxious about anything, but in every situation, by prayer and petition, with thanksgiving, present your requests to God."

This is so deep! It may seem impossible when you are in the middle of breaking down and are anxious about something that is not forthcoming, and yet you still have to be patient? Yes, be patient, and you will surely smile at the end. Remember patience is not just waiting, but your attitude while waiting that makes a difference.

I will share my own experience recently with the Department of Motor Vehicles (DMV) and United Postal Services (UPS). If you live in Houston, Texas, you will understand exactly what I'm talking about, our patience is being tested every day, and it allows us to actually know our strengths and weaknesses.

Due to Covid-19, it was really difficult getting into many places. I made an appointment to have a name change at the DMV, which apparently took two months to process. I got there on my appointment day and I did not have an original document, just the photocopy. I tried explaining with one million reasons why I didn't have the original document needed, but none of my explanations attracted any sympathy from the lady assisting me. I was close to losing my mind, so I asked what then do I do ma'am?

It took me two months to get this appointment and her reply was, you need to go back and book another appointment."

She didn't even allow me to go home and grab the original document, which was really frustrating, and I took the blame. I should have double checked my document, right? We left, and I made another appointment, and this time it took me three months, which is not a big deal, I guess. When it was time, I made sure I grabbed as much documentation as I could - all of the files in the house that had both my maiden name and my marital name. When I arrived to the DMV, first thing was to get screened, and then you have to check in. I checked in, and my husband checked in a few minutes before me. My number was closer than my husband's, and we waited about thirty minutes, and when it got to my number, I was skipped. They called the number before and after mine, and I was left there sitting and wondering, not again. My husband's number was called fifteen minutes later, and I am still sitting, so I decided to go and ask why I was skipped.

I approached the first lady, and said, "Good Morning." She responded, "How can I help you?"

So I said, "Ma'am, sorry to bother you, I was just wondering how I was skipped?"

She replied with, "You need to go back to your seat and wait for your number to be called."

At that point, I lost it. I smiled and returned to my seat. Once my number was finally called, it was more drama with my documents. My point here is that sometimes we are in a situation where it seems that no one cares or understands you. Everyone is lacking empathy, and you know you can't control the situation. Just sit back and be patient, there is no need to be frustrated.

We have seen a lot of people who went through a lot in life, and we need to learn from some of their experiences. The point is that God will always put some challenging situations on us, and things will not always go the way we want them to, but please remember patience is the key.

Everything you are going through is preparing you for what you asked God for. If you don't want your patience to be tested, stop asking God for patience, because it is then that all temptations of losing patience will come in.

Remember this today, as long as you wake up every day, it is a sign that God is not through with you yet, and his plan for you has not been accomplished. You may be feeling miserable and living with no purpose, trust God and put Him first in everything you do. He will direct you, correct you and make you humble. God is good, and he is everything we need.

PEACE IN A TIME OF STORM

This is a promise from God that he will give us his peace during our darkest moments. Sounds quite unrealistic, right? Yeah, but it's true! When God promises us anything, he never fails. When He was preparing his followers, He promised them that the Holy Spirit will be with them to comfort and give them peace. Those words are still alive today. Just as life throws many challenges at us each day, we need to keep reminding ourselves about this promise: that the storm will not kill you or steal your joy.

God has not forgotten you. Put a smile on your face and keep the faith, don't be consumed by what God is doing in someone else's life. Focus on the promises of God in your own life. You are so important because of the price that was made to you on the cross.

My niece was heartbroken, One faithful day she got a call that changed her whole life, and that call will never be forgotten for as long as she lives. Sadly, the call was from her daughter's daycare where she normally takes her every day before work. The baby had no signs of sickness, no allergies, no previous medical conditions or medical issues. She went to her normal doctor's appointment, which had not displayed any red flags, she was a healthy beautiful little princess.

After feeding the baby they said she started crying nonstop, so the lady called my niece and advised her to take the baby to a hospital for care or call the emergency line, which they did, but before her mom got there, she was gone. The poor baby had passed away.

No time to say goodbye to her loving charming little girl, just the beautiful kiss she received from her before dropping her off at the daycare. It's the most painful when you do not have the chance to hold or whisper your last words, she never knew when she was dropping her child off to the daycare that day that it would be her last moment with her, but when you believe in God you will understand that loss is only temporary. Sadly enough, she died only a few days prior to her one year birthday, the little girl was taken by her creator when it most pleased him.

God allowed this to happen for different reasons which cannot be questioned, which may cause pain, but it is necessary for our growth. It's difficult and overwhelming to choose peace when life throws so many questions and unforgettable memories at us, but we need not to faint but be courageous. Your miracle is not on what you lost, but what is left.

If you ever needed it, you would not have lost it. Remember, when you allow God to step into situations such as this, miracles happens. The battles of life knows how to deal with people, regardless of who you are, it does not miss anyone's address. It could be worse than a woman who lost a child.

But we have a God who cares and knows how you feel and how hurtful and heartbroken you are' relax and trust him.

TEN
YEAR
WAIT
AND
THEY
CHOSE
PEACE

Here's a story of a couple who have been asking God for a child for many years and married for over ten years. Back home in Africa, having kids after marriage is a big deal. There is a lot of expectations and pressures, not only from your spouse, who basically understands your fears and troubles, but also from your family members. This lady had peace that one day she would be able to prove that she is capable of producing offspring. The test results from the doctors showed that she is barren, meaning she was unproductive, unfruitful. Also, age was contributing to her infertility.

The family is anxious to hear a baby's cry and have their great expectation fulfilled. Year after year she had been threatened so many times by her husband's family, that they needed to choose another wife for her husband, because she was not able to reproduce. In the midst of this, she had peace that Gods time is the best, and she knew that she would be called a mother someday. Her heart was open to receive and love. Her imagination wondered constantly about how lovely and beautiful her kids will look. Her grief never ended; she cried day and night for help and hoping GOD will answer her prayers in this hard time. Each day it seemed she had lost it, but there was something she was confident about during this hard time of wait, which was the peace from God. You cannot trade that for anything, God uses time of waiting to stretch our faith and belief.

This couple had peace that God is never late and has not brought them this far to abandon them. They refused to believe the physical report from the doctors who can only do their best professionally but have no idea about divine miracles. They believed that their cry and prayers are not useless in the sight of God. Most of the time God waits until the last minutes to show his glory, and this will blow your mind.

One day the long-awaited time came, and their whole world was changed. Here comes this unusual sickness, remember, not only was she declared barren but also her age was close to menopause which makes the possibility of getting pregnant low. Based on human belief or speculation, it looks completely impossible for someone at her age to be pregnant, but that did not steal her peace. So she called her usual doctor to have herself examined, and the results came out that she was pregnant!

You may have experienced several times where God chooses to take you through the longer route just to build you up and make you stronger. Hebrew 10:36 says, "We can only receive God's promises if we are patient enough to do his will."

God allows suffering to come our way for a specific reason, and this couple refused to descend to the way their family were thinking and acting with unbelief, because they know that God will surely fulfill his promise.

H

O

P

E

You have to be strong in faith and filled with positivity to see light despite the darkness surrounding you, in other to succeed with the struggle of life you need to build your confidence to deal with whatever circumstances you face in life

Hoping to see light in the darkness is another example of FAITH that makes you stronger. Hoping for divine transformation and believing it will happen even when it feels like your life is falling apart, so stay unshakable because the reality you are hoping for may just be around the corner' your better days are coming.

God will show you exactly what he has for you in a clear and uninterrupted note. Just listen and pay more attention to his voice. A greater tomorrow, despite the circumstance. Be hopeful and confident.

To accomplish this great tomorrow it's very smart not to share your dreams or what you hope for with the wrong people, because all they will end up doing is discouraging you, laughing at you, and even call you names. Have you ever asked why you have desired to be successful in life?

Dreaming of having the best? We as people have dreams but not equally, only few live to see their dreams come to reality. Let your story be different, get started as GOD will definitely keep showing you what you are capable of, you just have to stay focused and live your life with great expectations, and this will surely come your way.

Hope is having the feeling that even though it tarries, it will come to pass. With God, everything is possible. You can face your fears and approach the future with the mindset that your efforts will have a positive impact.

Having the belief that this circumstance will be better, no doubt that it will be better' when your hope is strong in God and your confidence is unshaken.

Taking our early life experience as an example, when growing up as a child you have this visions and hopes to become somebody in the future. You could be very wealthy and successful, or someone who will never quits no matter what life throws at them. The vision was clear, but there are lots of challenges discouraging the vision, for those who were born without a golden spoon will understand better.

Having to grow up in a family where the only way to survive is farming and most of the time you have to complete your homework in the early morning before thinking of going to school. A situation where you have only one notebook for four lessons, sometimes no breakfast before school, and even when you return from school there's still no lunch. Despite all these challenges you still hope that it will get better one day, you never stop pushing on getting the vision to actualize.

Hope comforts you to stay focused and stronger. What is it that you are hoping for?

The situation can change overnight, but this can happen only when you have a mindset that it will change. If you fall five times, rise up six times. One day, everything will make perfect sense to you.

Miracles happen! I have seen so many people who at the time of losing hope, everything changes. Their whole life has a total turnaround because God has a clear vision of what tomorrow holds.

Are you wondering when this will be over? Don't be dismay. Every unpleasant situation is temporary. Let's be glad and rejoice each day and rest assured that the best day is ahead, even when we don't have any idea of what tomorrow will bring. Just be positive, hope for the best, be strong and it will surely get better. Remember, just as there's time for everything, so will your time of hoping and believing come to pass. You may have been discouraged about life, stop at this moment and remember that the road to success is not smooth and is not going to always be smooth. You need to focus more on gratitude and appreciate God for today and the challenges.

My brother was infected with an unknown disease for years, it was so scary each time this unpleasant condition would come. We had been looking for a solution from every angle of life, both medical, spiritual, and traditional, but no solution was found. On many occasions, we have had spiritual herbalist do cleansing on him, which was suggested from people who believed this may be the cure. We lost hope and were confident that things would never be the same.

It's scary that when this attack would come, he will lose his senses, acting as if he was possessed or like someone who is being controlled by a demon, some people called it a demonic attack. All kinds of names have been given to this sickness.

I remember one night I was sleeping with my mom, and we heard this loud scream from the other room. My brother was sleeping, we woke up and ran to him and we found him holding the window burglar rails, he was pulling it and screaming with fear. I was crying with my mom, we couldn't control the situation nor were we able to bring him down, I ran out calling for help in the middle of the night, sometimes at 1 am.

My mom and I were so confused. She was crying and yelling for help too. When I went outside, I saw a cat by the same window my brother was pulling, trying to come out, at that moment I almost fainted, fear grabbed me, but I didn't stop yelling for help. I remember praying and rebuking the cat, I called out for Jesus like a million times and people from the community came out to our rescue. They helped us to bring him down and to administer some holy water that we had.

Holy water is water that was blessed in the church.

This condition had been on and on for years and sometimes I just stopped believing things will ever be okay with my brother. I know a lot of people may be going through worse situations, but we need not faint or be weary, the devil will not take the glory. Build your confidence in God, who knows everything about you from the beginning.

I have had several doctors come check up on him, in hopes to find a solution. One day, I got a call from my family that it had started again, I cried at work and everyone knew something was wrong with me. Money was not an issue at this point, anytime I was asked to bring anything I was always providing, I spent all my savings and so did my siblings. One of the occasions I asked them to take him to a hospital called UBTH, a teaching hospital in Benin Edo state Nigeria. Were they carried a series of test.

After many tests and evaluations, he was diagnosed with Epilepsy. Doctors were confused because Epilepsy can happen at any time of the day and anywhere. Epilepsy is also not limited to when you can get the incision, for my brother the incision only occurred when he was sleeping. We did everything humanly possible to get an answer but no avail, until one day he was prescribed a medication that has been helping reduce the incision. I told him that the only solution is God, this battle belonged to God, and that he needed to rededicate his life totally to God. He created him in his likeness, so if it pleases Him to have him die out of his circumstances, we will accept it by faith. His life belongs to Him.

God has been good, and I am telling this story to let someone know that God is never late in any situation or circumstance, no matter how terrible the condition may seem. It has been almost a year now and he has never experienced any discomfort, and I still believe God was responsible for total healing. Never give up when waiting, God shows up at his own time. It was really a heartbreaking time for my mom and siblings. Watching him suffer from this horrible situation sounds like a movie, right? Trust me, this is reality.

At a point, he was considering committing suicide as his life was completely different. With this scary sickness, people wouldn't associate with him as if he had control over the sickness, and he couldn't get a good job because his physical appearance was discouraging, looking like a mentally disordered man on the street. He could go days without eating or associating with anyone.

Your situation may be worst, but God is not done with you yet. When God is finished with you at his own time, you will be like a tree planted by the riverside. All that you have ever lost over the years will be recovered, but this will happen if only you believe and hope that it will happen, be positive minded.

What you put out is what will come back to you. You can't plant corn and expect it to germinate orange or mango. Let your hope be strong, so when temptation comes you will not be moved. Condition your mind for positivity and remember our minds operate at different levels, positive or negative, don't give room to the wrong side of it.

Sometimes we hear people say I don't know how I feel today, feels like I woke up on the wrong side of the bed. At that moment negativity will set in. And you tend to condition our mind that today will not be a good day, the devil then has the opportunity to elaborate on that and have your day messed up for you. You are in charge of how your mind operates, you should always expect to have a great day. Prophecy to have a good thing happen, at this moment your mind starts sending signals to your thoughts that there is no room for negativity.

Everything is going to be okay, maybe not today, but eventually it will. Trust God and hold fast to your hope, your flesh may fail, but God will not. During these difficult times, it's easy to panic and conclude all hope is gone, and we let fear come in which will destroy you more and make you lose confidence. Just be strong and remember everything is going to be fine, God's love has consumed us so much that fear and anxiety cannot overtake us.

Let your prayers each day be:

Dear God, if today I lose my hope, please remind me that your plans are better than my fears.

When confronted with disappointment, just find hope in God. Are you wondering when your time will come? It is now. When you believe and hope in him who has the final words (GOD).

God will turn the trials you face today into triumph, your mess, into an everlasting message. Are you a victim of something you know nothing about? You will be victorious. Hope is the conviction that something will turn out well.

HIS GRACE FOUND ME

It's a mystery how God's Grace always comes at a time when we least expect. Like the wind, His grace finds us even when we least expected it, when we are blinded and consumed with disobedience, He still loves and crowns us with His Love. I remember one day, I was speaking with my boss about life and how privileged we were. Then I heard that soft voice saying, "Have you mentioned how I loved you and gifted you with grace, or the place you were when grace found you?"

Immediately I broke down and started crying, "GOD, I will testify of your goodness and share my gratitude to your people, and for those who might have lost their hope." God's grace is abundant and always available to those who need it. Get prepared for He is about to take you to another level in your life. He will make everything beautiful in his time.

I was like a living being without direction. When in my deepest poverty, He brought me out. As a child, I was not privileged to live the best life or have what my friends had. I remember how I would occasionally go to someone's houses on a Sunday morning, helping with their house chores just to be able to eat rice and source, which was really big deal then - especially when you grow up in a remote area or environment. Those who were born without the golden spoon will catch the gist.

Sometimes, people will take advantage of you and put their own kid's responsibilities on you, such as cleaning and washing clothes by hand. The worst is grinding their tomatoes and peppers with the local grinding stone. When the grace of God found me, I knew it, things began to fall in place for me, and everything I layed my hands on became productive and successful.

I kept the struggle real and was really energetic and optimistic about my future and my greatness. I graduated from the university and had two jobs waiting for me. My husband, Daniel, was also my backbone and a blessing to me, he knew what I would become just by seeing the positive energy I had. I had never allowed my status to define me. Daniel stood by me; several times he sold his personal belongings just to make sure I was taken care of.

The most amazing and life-changing story was when I got a visa lottery to the United States, without me applying for the lottery. It all just happened because of his grace. Someone had played the lottery for over two thousand students, of which I was one of the two lucky ones that were chosen without my knowledge. What else can you call it but grace? When it's time for God to favor you, it doesn't matter where you are, your grace will locate you.

I am saying this to encourage you that all you need in life to succeed is divine grace. Just right after I graduated, I changed my cellphone number, just hoping to start a new life, but I have always had my husband's number as an alternative number. So when this guy who played the lottery was looking for me because my phone had been disconnected and he didn't even know me, he reached out to my alternative number, and it was my husband. He asked for me, and it was confirmed I have gone for my national youth service, they both agreed to meet, just to be sure of the authenticity of the visa, and that it was a real lottery.

This was the beginning of my life-changing story. Don't be depressed or frustrated about any situation. You may think that you're not good enough, but God's grace and love is bigger than who you think you are in the world.

God of grace will be gracious to you, here I am today because of grace, such an imperfect soul that he chose to show mercy to. Faithful and merciful Father, trust in him and his grace and your life will never be the same again. All of your days have already been written in God's book, so when you go through disappointment and frustration don't stop there, keep moving and believe in him. You will be tired, discouraged and frustrated, don't give up on the future because he was faithful yesterday, today and he will still be tomorrow and forever.

God's grace carried me here, and his grace is greater than any circumstance or addiction in your life. Don't be afraid of your challenges because the bigger the challenges you have, the greater the grace of God is for you. He giveth more grace when the burden is stronger. His grace has no measure or limits, neither does his power have any boundaries. I was filled and consumed with sin and poverty, but he covered me with his immeasurable grace. This same power and love are still much available for anyone. He gives us the willingness to help us do what we could never do on our own. It's called unmerited favor from God and so much more. I encourage you to be grateful for what you have and where you are today, don't take anything for granted, and live life to the fullest.

People tend to allow all of the negative experiences in their life to mess up their mind or spoil their mood and all the good stuff that they had, forgetting the great moments and all the beautiful things around them. Relax and take a break and ponder on the good things that will supersede the negativity.

When God decided to favor you, he will start showing you mercy, and each moment of your life will be filled with testimony; everything will begin to fall in place. All you need is to believe and stand upright, you can't experience this unprecedented divine favor with doubt and disbelief I would cry day and night when I lost hope, but when I realize the power of Gods words and his promises, I stuck to it and asked for his mercy. He says to Moses in Romans 9:15: "I will have mercy to whom I will have mercy, and compassion on whom I will have compassion."

That could be you today, so why weary? It may not come now, just hold on. I would constantly remind myself of great people who had a turnaround and transformation because they realized who they are and cry for mercy - Jabez, Blind Bartimus.

God does not qualify you by your righteousness, how rich or poor you are, your background, race, or status. He chooses to show mercy on who he chooses, let that be your story today. People who look down on you will be surprised and will be consumed with confusion trying to figure out what happened. I was not perfect but was hoping that a day will come when he who is perfect will change my life, and it happened. Get yourself up and start acting and believing like one who is loaded with everything you need.

Many people are currently living in an unimaginable situation, when you have the opportunity to meet them, you will no longer only cry for yourself.

After I graduated from the university, it was a privilege to serve my country for one year, which is called NYSC (National Youth Service Corp). I was deployed to a specific state for service. I would have never believed there was a place like this. No words or conviction would have been enough for me to believe humans can live in that kind of situation or environment. Believe me, it's horrible and the scariest places I have ever been.

People live in deep poverty, uncivilized, with no

electricity or even grocery stores. The kids sit on the floor in schools, of which we had to go to their houses sometimes to bring them to school.

We would basically travel hours to the local county to buy our daily necessities once a month.

The only means of transportation out of this place are vehicles that transport cows, camel, and bags of grains. We sat with animals in trucks just to be able to move around.

I was not having it, but other corps members were seeing it as fun and taking each day as it comes.

My first day was a life and death situation. My skin changed, my lips were cracked and burnt because of the hot weather, no air condition, and no window. Not to mention the restrooms.

My point here is we need not to complain about what is not working out for us or our current suffering, instead, be appreciative for every day, and you will find favor one day.

The worst of the nightmare is having to drink water that is totally brown. It's clear and clean the moment you're fetching the water, and once it settles the color changes, turning brown and disgusting. I remember my colleagues were making fun of me, "Martha, you need to snap out of this and accept the fact that we are stuck here for one year."

This community had only one water generating source for everyone in that community that needed water… What a sad story. Of course, we were given the opportunity to come to the water stations twice a day, so we don't have to wait in line with the community people.

We made covers for the doors and windows for safety. I am encouraging you today to see the light and hope in your situation. One day, I was cooking, and suddenly people from the community gathered and were staring at me, looking all confused. I asked what the problem was, then a friend named Musa who happened to understand a little English helped me understand the situation at hand. Musa was always around us, helping with different things and interpreting their language.

I asked, "Musa, why is everyone here, looking all confused?"

Musa replied, "They smelled the aroma from the food."

"What?" I almost broke down.

"The aroma is unusual for them."

"You must be joking, sounds funny to me."

So I decided to share the food (plantains)I was cooking among them' so they can have a taste of it, instead of eating the skin that was peeled off of it' as they have asked if they can have the plantain skin. In few seconds, they were eating on it, I am sure your situation and pain isn't as bad as this, right?

Worse experience in this community.'
Snakes and scorpions move around like they are

family members.

One day, I said to myself, "I am done, I can't stand this anymore, and I need to move to the state capital. I left for months, which felt like a whole lifetime. We climbed on trees to hang our cell phones just to receive or send text messages to family and friends, with no internet. We managed to buy a small power generator to help charge our phones and laptops so we could play music.

Each time I get discouraged; I remember those people. They were so happy and saw nothing wrong with their living conditions. They just saw it as a normal life, they were always joyful.

We managed to stay until the end of our service time, and thereafter, I heard they no longer posted anyone to that community. I pray and ask that God will always remember these people and bring them more joy and light.

The mercy of God changes all situations. He will restore all you have lost.

Martha A. Okwuokenye is based in Houston, Tx, and is married to Daniel Okwuokenye, with two handsome boys, Michael and Jaydan. She graduated from the University of Benin Edo State Nigeria, where she studied banking and finance.

Martha was inspired to write her first novel, "Worth More Than you Know", by her early life experiences, research, and struggles. She loves to inspire and motivate others through her writing and storytelling. Martha is an extremely confident person that always sees tomorrow as being bright. Her faith is very important to her, one of her mantras is, "No limitation will ever deprive me of achieving my Gods given purpose."

Martha hopes that her writing will inspire her readers to be grateful for what they have, who they are and what they are called to do.

"Keep pushing harder, be encouraged, and keep focused."

— Martha A. Okwuokenye

www.ingramcontent.com/pod-product-compliance
Lightning Source LLC
Chambersburg PA
CBHW071912070526
44583CB00016B/1962